DAVY CROCKETT

ELLIOT DOOLEY

Adapted by Dr. Marion Kimberly

GALLERY BOOKS
An Imprint of W. H. Smith Publishers Inc.
112 Madison Avenue
New York City 10016

© 1990 Ediciones B, S.A., Barcelona, Spain

This edition published 1991 by Gallery Books,
an imprint of W.H.Smith Publishers, Inc.,
112 Madison Avenue, New York, New York 10016

ISBN 0-8317-1461-1

Gallery Books are available for bulk purchase for sales
promotions and premium use. For details write or telephone
the Manager of Special Sales, W.H.Smith Publishers, Inc.,
112 Madison Avenue, New York, New York 10016. (212) 532-6600

Produced by Hawk Books Limited, London

Printed in Spain

Take that back, or else I'll . . .

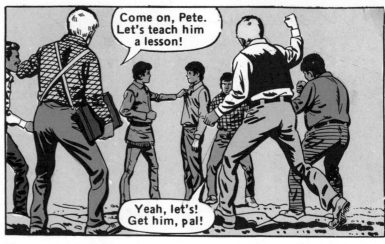

Come on, Pete. Let's teach him a lesson!

Yeah, let's! Get him, pal!

Let go of me! I'm not going to say it again! You cow herder!

You asked for it! Take that!

Ow!

I'll fix you, Davy Crockett! I'll tell my father.

So . . . Davy couldn't stay home and go to school. Pete's father was the most important man in town and . . .

What'll we do now, son? They're making life impossible for us.

I'm not sorry for what I did, Pa. I'll have to go away . . .

So, a little later . . .

God bless you, son. Take care of yourself.

And so, because of a fight, Davy Crockett had to leave home . . .

Can you give me a lift? I'm on my way to look for work.

Sure. Hop on.

I'm a peddler, and I'm on my way to Baltimore. You can come with me.

Baltimore? Yes. I've never been there. That would be fine.

Davy lived there for a year, doing odd jobs. Then one day . . .

Gee, I'd love to sail on one of those ships!

Boy, do you like the sea?

What?

I sure do! I've never sailed, but I'd love to try it . . .

Well, you've got the chance now. I'm leaving for Europe and I need a cabin boy. Want the job?

Do I ever! Do you mean it?

I don't say things I don't mean.

We'll never know if Davy Crockett would have made a good sailor, because . . .

Just a minute, Captain! You can't take this lad on as cabin boy! He's under age, and his parents wouldn't allow it.

Who is this man?

"He's from my home town, sir."

"Well, you are very young. He's right, your parents will be needing you. I'm sorry, but . . ."

"Wait a minute, please, Captain!"

So Davy lost the chance to go to sea. He was forced to move on again with only uncertain adventures ahead of him . . .

Again he worked at odd jobs . . .

"Giddap, mules! Push harder, Davy!"

Davy's great eagerness to learn never left him. Whenever he had a free moment . . .

Then one day he decided . . .

"Home! I'm going back to see my parents again!"

"With all the wild game around my home town, I could earn my living hunting and fur trapping . . ."

When he reached the cabin . . . "Davy, boy!" "Is it really you, Davy?"

"It's good to be home."

"You've changed so much, Davy!"

The town had changed too . . .

Who's that man?

That's Davy Crockett. He just came home.

Everything had changed except Pete's hate for Davy, all because of the fight they had long before . . .

Pete, Davy Crockett's back.

I know. And when I see him, I'm going to give him a fight for a welcoming present.

Ma, Pa, if I work as a trapper, I'll be able to pay my share.

Sounds like a good idea, Davy. I know you will succeed.

The next day Davy started out on his new life of trapping.

Ha! Come to catch some little rabbits?

Ho, ho! He'd better try just for squirrels!

Get out of town, Crockett. We don't want your kind around here.

He'd been insulted again! Davy's face flushed with anger. He was ready to teach Pete another lesson . . .

You'll eat those words, you miserable . . .

Suddenly they heard . . .

Did you hear that?

¡GRRRRR!

What on earth was it?

¡GRRRRR!

¡GRAUG!

Aaaaaw!

The man and the bear were so close that Davy couldn't shoot for fear of hitting Pete.

PETE!

Help! Help!

Hold on! I'll help you!

GRRRR!

Oh no! The bear will kill him!

DAVY!

Before he fell to the ground, dead, the bear clawed Davy Crockett's arm.

You saved my life, Crockett!

I'm really sorry that I made fun of him.

We should help him. He's badly hurt!

Staggering from his wound, Davy went to a nearby cabin for help.

I need help . . .

When he woke up a few hours later, he was in bed . . .

Relax, you are among friends. I'm Polly Finley.

You fainted just outside our door. We brought you in here.

Thank you, sir. I owe my life to you.

We've only done what any good neighbour would do.

Davy got well and returned to his hunting but he spent most of his free time at the Finley's cabin. Two years later . . .

I hope you'll be very happy, Polly.

Davy Crockett will be a fine husband!

And they were married that day.

I now pronounce you man and wife.

Davy and Polly lived in the Finley's cabin. In a few years they had two little boys.

Are you happy, Davy?

I have been since the day we got married.

Their happiness was interrupted one day when suddenly ...

Indians! The Indians are on the warpath! They're wearing warpaint.

Indians? What tribe?

The Creeks. General Jackson is asking for volunteers.

Later

Don't you see, Polly? The army will pay well for my services as a scout.

Oh Davy, we'll miss you so much!

It will only be for a while, honey. We can use the money to pay our debts. Then maybe someday we'll have our own home. We've got to think of the children, Polly.

Finally, the next day ...

Goodbye, my loved ones. I'll be back.

Two weeks after entering the army as a scout, Davy was called . . .

Bring the new scout, Davy Crockett, to me.

Yes, sir, right away.

You want to see me, General?

Yes, Crockett. Come here.

First, I want to welcome you, Crockett. We need men like you in the army.

It is my duty, sir.

Tomorrow you will go on a scouting mission with your friend, Russell. Be careful!

You can count on me, General.

In the morning . . .

Hold on! Those tracks are Indian footprints!

Moments later . . .

You're right, Davy. The Creeks are advancing.

Go back and tell the General. I'll keep watch here.

He's bound to see me!

Ooo...

There was no choice. Davy did what had to be done.

¡BANG!

Look! Over there!

FASTER!

Russell hurried back to the fort to warn General Jackson . . .

FORWARD!

BANG!

Stop where you are! One step closer and this brave will die!

Quickly, Davy . . .

. . . mounted his horse and headed at a gallop for the fort. On the way he saw a troop of soldiers . . .

Russell made it. Good! I'm glad to see you! The Indians are right behind me.

Thanks, Crockett. Where are they? We'll attack at once!

The Indians and soldiers fought fiercely.

It ended with a victory for Jackson over the Creeks. When they returned, the General called Davy to his office . . .

You're the man I need to look for Chief Black Eye. We want him to sign a peace treaty.

Do you know Black Eye? He's powerful and cunning. He and his Creek warriors haven't been defeated yet, not by a long shot, Crockett.

You're right, General. After all, they're fighting for their land. There must be some way to work it out so we don't have to keep killing each other.

The government plans to set aside land for the Indians where they can live peacefully. But the Indians aren't satisfied with that.

I understand, sir. When do I leave?

Tomorrow at dawn. Take two scouts from your group with you.

Davy chose Russell and another good friend of his called "Old Lonely". They set out the next day . . .

Keep your eyes open! We'll run into Black Eye's men any time now. Remember, we want to talk not fight.

Davy's shots were heard . . .

Who could have fired those shots? I don't like this at all.

Shots! That's bad! Something must have happened to one of the others.

What?

Old Lonely wasn't far from Russell and . . .

Indians! They've got Russell!

Stop it! Get your hands off me! I'll fight you all!

Davy heard Russell's shouting. A few minutes later . . .

Where's Russell?

They jumped him and took him prisoner.

I could do nothing against so many.

You did the right thing. They'd have gotten you too. Russell needs both of us to get him out of this mess . . .

What's your plan?

I'll challenge Black Eye to a fight. If I win, maybe he'll sign the peace treaty and let Russell go.

The Indian code of honor will make Black Eye accept my challenge so he won't look like a coward in front of his warriors.

Two hours later . . .

Well, there's Black Eye's camp. You wait here and cover me. We may have to shoot our way out if i haven't figured this right.

Be careful, Davy. Good luck!

Later

I come in peace. Tell Black Eye that Davy Crockett wants to have a pow-wow with him.

What do you want, Paleface?

For you to smoke the peace pipe with me and have our people be friends.

Paleface always lie. Me no trust.

The best proof that I'm sincere is that I'm here, Black Eye. I want nothing but peace.

You leave now, Paleface.

No, Black Eye. I never run away. When I have to, I can fight. I'll show you if you want. Come on, Black Eye!

Davy had been careful enough in his challenge to go far enough, but not too far . . .

Who you want to fight?

I challenge you Black Eye! What do you say?

Black Eye looked sideways at his men. He knew that he couldn't refuse Davy's challenge.

I accept, Paleface. You die at my hands!

Just a minute! If I win, my prize is to be peace among our peoples and the life of my friend Russell, the man you've taken prisoner.

I agree, Paleface. But I will win, and you will have no peace. Then Russell will die too.

Half an hour later, in the middle of the camp . . .

The important fight began!

As Davy was knocked to the ground, all the warriors let out a cry that showed they thought the fight was about to end.

But Davy jumped to his feet and . . .

Ahhhh!

The Indian braves were very still as they awaited what they thought would be the death of their chief, but . . .

I have won the right to kill your chief. I'm not going to do it. I want peace between our peoples. Do you understand?

Davy's noble gesture won the admiration of the Indians.

Black Eye believes the Paleface is sincere. We will smoke peace pipe, and Russell will be set free.

And so, thanks to Davy Crockett's courage and daring, General Jackson got the peace treaty he wanted so badly.

You have my thanks, Davy. The army and the nation will never forget all you've done.

A few days later . . .

Crockett returned to his home and the life of a hunter and trapper.

BANG!

He provided well for his family and they lived comfortably.

As the time passed, he was made a local judge. One day when he was in the town bar with some neighbours . . .

Judge Crockett, I need your help. I have to arrest a very dangerous man.

I'll come with you, Sheriff.

Thanks, Judge. Keep your eyes open.

A few minutes later, the Sheriff and Davy Crockett cornered the bandit . . .

What?

In the name of the law, you're under arrest. Your gun slinging days are over.

Simmons reached for his gun, and . . .

You really think so, Sheriff?

But then . . .

Uhhh!

Okay, you've got your man, Sheriff. Lock him up, and we'll give him a trial.

That was only one of Davy's brave deeds. After a while these deeds made him famous for miles around. And so one day . . .

We came to ask you if you'd be willing to run for Congress from this state, Mr. Crockett.

Me, in Congress? What is this, a joke?

But Davy did run for Congress in 1827 in Tennessee, and he was elected. One day on the floor of the House . . .

Gentlemen, this law you're suggesting is an insult to the Indians.

Crockett is blocking our laws which protect the settlers.

He's nothing but a dreamer.

This law would break the peace with the Indians. They respect treaties. They have a right to live, just as we have.

Davy Crockett's words were heard all over the country. But soon he was home again . . .

I never want to go back to Congress, Polly. I want to be a hunter and live here quietly with you.

I'm going up the Red River and try to reach the territory of Texas. I hear there's good hunting out that way and lots of money to be made.

I knew you'd go there one day, Davy.

A few days later . . .

Be careful, Davy. Write me as soon as you arrive.

See you soon, honey.

A few hours later . . .

There the paleface, Crockett!

On your horses.

Suddenly Davy turned his head and saw . . .

Giddap, there. We have visitors.

Wouldn't that be something! After defending Indian rights in Congress, to be killed by Indians in these hills . . .

But Davy was wrong about the Indians.

We come in peace, Crockett. We want to speak with you.

Davy stopped . .

We want to thank you for all you've done for us, Davy Crockett.

The truth is, my friends, I was able to do very little.

The men in Congress didn't want to listen to me. They passed many laws that are bad for you. I'm really sorry.

We know which side you're on. Our people are poor and hungry. But you did what you could, and we want you to know that you have our gratitude.

As Davy said his farewell to the Indians, he had the satisfaction of knowing that he was not being blamed for their troubles.

Your words comfort me. Go in peace. Good hunting!

Soon he arrived in Fulton, where . . .

I'll grab a ride on that steamboat.

Once on board . . . Well, if that isn't Davy Crockett, the former Congressman!

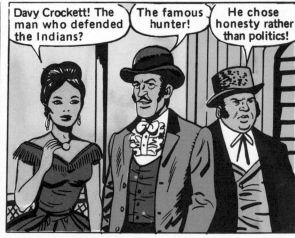

Davy Crockett! The man who defended the Indians?

The famous hunter!

He chose honesty rather than politics!

Excuse me, Mr. Crockett, but I'd very much like to meet you. My name is Thimberling. I've followed your political career with great interest.

My political career was very short, Mr. Thimberling. You're very kind.

I always admired you, Mr. Crockett.

Thimberling and Davy Crockett became good friends and decided to travel to Texas together.

Davy also met a man named Johnson on the boat. When it docked . . .

Thanks to you, I enjoyed the ride.

Why don't we travel together for a while?

Crockett was headed for a wooded region rich in game. But after a few days, near the city of San Antonio . . .

Well I'll be! That looks like an uprising.

Davy was right. Trouble was brewing . . .

What's going on here?

Haven't you heard? We're fighting for the independence of Texas.

All the townspeople had taken up arms to fight . . .

It's war! We're fighting for the right of Texas to be free.

What do you think, Davy? They're at war with Mexico.

At that moment, in another part of the city . . .

And they say they just saw Davy Crockett?

Yes, Mr. President, he's here in Texas.

A man with Crockett's reputation would be useful to our cause.

Bring him here! Tell him that the President of Texas, Sam Houston, wants to see him.

And that was how, a few hours later . . .

I spend my days now hunting and being a farmer. But you can count on my complete cooperation in your fight to free Texas.

What about my two friends?

Ask them to join us in the fight for an independent Texas. We need good men.

The next day General Santa Anna led his Mexican Army in an attack . . .

We'll bury those Texans! Forward!

The Mexicans attacked . . .

MEXICANS! Fall back!

Retreat!

To the Alamo!

They're tearing the city apart, Captain.

Keep firing! Don't leave anyone alive!

Texas independent, eh? Ho, ho!

Meanwhile . . .

Well, Crockett, we can't hold off the whole Mexican army.

We won't give up, Mr. President.

We can hole up in the Alamo and let them try to get us out. That's what I'd do.

The Alamo, an old Franciscan mission, became a fort for the Texans' last stand, a battle which has become a legend.

Sam Houston, with Davy Crockett!

A few days later . . .

They've all taken refuge in the Alamo, General.

Is that so?

They just want to frighten us. They know that as long as we hold this fort, Texas won't be theirs.

You're right, Crockett.

Dig in for the defence, Colonel. We're going down fighting.

Then the cannons started roaring. The Mexicans would spare nothing to take this fort.

BOOOOM!

To your posts! Stop the attack!

Now, Crockett. You take charge of the defence.

Forward!

The fort is ours!

Let's find Davy. Right about now he may need some help.

Don't let up! Keep shooting!

Time and again the Mexicans were turned back.

Sam Houston, you must leave the Alamo or you will be trapped. After this fight Texas will need its President.

Against his will, Houston was persuaded. He left the Alamo at dawn the next day. Forty-eight hours later he formally announced the independence of Texas.

Houston asks us to hold out until he can send help. He is forming an army.

A little later, the Mexican troops, knowing they must destroy the Alamo or lose Texas . . .

Attack!

CLOSE YOUR RANKS!

Ugh!

Thimberling! Johnson!

Davy ran to find his friends, but he was too late . . .

They're both dead!

Meanwhile, very near the Alamo, General Santa Anna said to his troops . . .

We are not going to stay here forever. It's time to finish off these Texans, once and for all!

Increase the shelling! RAPID FIRE!

The Mexican Army poured a rain of shells upon the fort. Afterwards . . .

CHARGE! Finish them off! The Alamo is ours!

After them!

After that shelling rain not even a rattlesnake could be left alive.

But General Santa Anna had not counted on the courage of the defenders of the Alamo.

Surrender or die!

CRUNCH!

Hit savagely on the back of the head, Davy Crockett fell to the ground, fatally wounded.

AAH!

A few moments later...

Little was left standing at the old Franciscan mission. The men who defended the Alamo are part of history now.

They were brave men! We will always remember this day and the men who defended the Alamo!

THE END

So the historic battle of the Alamo was over. And the adventurous life of the brave Davy Crockett was ended also. But his name lives on in American legend.